REMOVE *the* STONES

TRACY WARREN

REMOVE THE STONES
Written By: Tracy Warren

TRU Statement Publications supports the right to free expression and the value of copyright. The purpose of copyright is to encourage writers and artist to produce the creative works that will leave a timeless impression of humanity.

The scanning, uploading, and distribution of this book without written permission is a theft of the author's intellectual property. If you would like permission to use materials from the book (other than for a review), please contact:
tracywarren78@yahoo.com
Thank you for your support of the author's rights.

Unless otherwise stated, all scripture quotations of the Holy Bible have been taken from the King James Version (KJV)

Cover photograph by © sveta, Adobe Stock
Cover photograph by © Jag_cz, Adobe Stock

Book Completion Services Provided by:
TRU Statement Publications
www.trustatementpublications.com

Copyright © 2021 Tracy Warren
First Edition: April 2021
Printed in the United States of America
0 4 1 3 2 0 2 1
ISBN: 978-1-948085-51-9

DEDICATIONS

This book is dedicated to my Mom Helen Trotter (rest peacefully), my husband who continues to encourage me, my kids, and grandkids.

To the people who have ever had stones that appeared to be walls in their lives and felt they could not overcome, I am a living witness that if you allow God to order your steps, then you can and you will OVERCOME.

Most importantly, this book is dedicated to my heavenly Father, for without Him and the intercession of Jesus I would not have lived to write this book. I am so grateful that He saw the best in me.

Philippians 4:13 ~ I can do all things through Christ which strengthened me.

CONTENTS

Foreword i

Remove The Stone 1

Remove The Stones of Fear 9

Remove The Stone of Bitterness 15

Remove The Stones of Jealousy 21

Remove The Stones of Anger 27

Remove The Stones of Self Righteousness 31

Remove The Stones of Hurt 35

Remove The Stones of False Humility 41

Be Desperate to Remove the Stones 47

FOREWORD

The Black woman is the most misunderstood being on planet earth. Their potential and perseverance is sometimes lost in their strength and not connected to the grace and sacrifice. My wife of seventeen years has shown me that we all have stones in our lives that have to be removed. This book, *Remove The Stones*, will bless you with the understanding that each move in your life was ordained to bring Glory to God.

It is stated that we are free will human beings, but you will see that you are more than that. We have dominion and power. This book was gracefully written by my wife, Tracy Warren. This book's timing will bless each person who ever questioned or asked God, *why?*

Elder Curtis Warren (Husband)
Kingdom Citizen Ministries Pastor

REMOVE THE STONES

1

REMOVE THE STONES

Back in 2009, the Lord gave me the name of this book, *Remove The Stones*, but I first thought it was a sermon that I was to preach until I fought, and couldn't come up with the sermon. As time went on, and mostly during my times of sitting trying to hear from the Lord, *Remove the Stones* would come, and it would go. I could remember some places and situation that came and went, and it left me feeling some type of way in my spirit man.

There were so many days when things occurred and I heard in my spirit the Lord say *I had no control over people*. But as time went on, it slowly came to me. I had met many people. People of God and others who I had high expectations of, only to be let down, disgraced, and put to shame as I was learning to *put not my trust in man*.

REMOVE THE STONES

Put not your trust in princes, nor in the son of man whom there is no help. ~Psalm 146:3

In this journey called life, there are many things that come to test you, things that come to shake you, things that come to move you, things that come to build you, things that come to uproot you, and things that come to shift you and if you're not grounded and rooted in the word of God that is just what can happen — all of thee above.

I had to learn lessons. And as you can see, I said *lessons* because things never stopped coming. I had to learn to deal with things and keep it moving. I learned the hard way that I wasn't at Burger King and I couldn't have things my way. I could remember times of being desperate for friends or people, only to attract all the wrong people. I really didn't know, I just wanted to be a part of the people of God.

I was a new convert, and I was on fire for the Lord. All of my blood family at the time, except for my mother, really didn't want to be bothered with me because I was saved and I was spitting— that's right, I said it *spitting* — fire and brimstones.

I could remember going through things and

having encounters that literally shook me, and I didn't know what I was going to do. In one incident I could remember being at my kids' ball game with my husband at the time, who is not my husband now. We were going through a divorce, and to me it seemed as if this divorce was dragging on and on. But in the midst of the divorce, we decided to reconcile for the sake of the kids, or so I thought.

We, women, have an intuition that is so accurate at times, and sometimes we have to learn to listen to our hearts. My husband, who was a drug dealer as well as a working guy (to call that a double business owner, per se), was going with a woman who he previously told me that he had broken it off with; well, that wasn't true.

So, while at my kids' ball game, I came out to the game and the woman and her sister were outside the door, parked right where I couldn't have missed them.

If I would have been thinking, I would have seen the plot and the plan of the enemy to take my life. But I was a new convert and had no guidance. People of God, it's important to have a mentor—Trust Me—they can help to give great counsel.

REMOVE THE STONES

Where no counsel is the people fall: but in the multitude of counsellors there is safety.
~Proverbs 11:14

At the time, I only had the bible that I was learning from and church on Sundays. At church I was told that I was a pretty young lady and the women in the church were ever so careful concerning me talking to the men or the pastor. So, I had no one to really talk to and guide me.

Well, at the ball game I was coming out of the door where the kids were playing ball to step out for a minute, and there was the enemy sitting and waiting. And as they were talking and moving their heads, so did I.

They jumped out the car, and we started to fight. It was two against one. As I begin to beat one of them out of their clothes, the other one began to stab me. I was stabbed twice in my back and once in my eye, and it was all over something that belonged to me by papers—I thought.

As weeks passed, I realized that he too was in on it, but hold on a minute that was not the worst part. The worst was I was thinking that God was going to avenge them in court. I was waiting on that court date because I just knew that God was going to fix everything. And guess what? That's not at all what happened; it actually went the other way.

I later found out that the woman worked for the judge. So instead of attempted murder, it was considered a simple assault. The judge held my case until the courtroom was empty and it was just the three of us. He humiliated me before my *then* husband and before my enemies. But in spite of it all, I still had hope in God.

Remember, I was a babe in Christ without any guidance. I had to gather my thoughts and keep my composure, because before giving my life to Christ, I was a fighter, but only if people did things to me. For the most part, I was now alone. My family lived in New Orleans, two hours away, and I didn't want to get them into any trouble, but there were many days when I thought that I was truly going to lose it.

My flesh and that old nature of mine was at war. I would wake up in the middle of the night with ideas of how to retaliate without getting caught. I mean, if the truth be told, I had already killed their entire family over and over in my mind; I just have to tell the truth. But as time went on, so did the thoughts. Even when I called myself casting every thought and imagination down that was not of God. And just let me say, this went on for years, but God is able to do everything but fail.

He brought me through those tough times and I slowly realize that it was not my battle, but this battle that I was fighting belongs to the Lord. I realize the plot the enemy had set didn't take me out, and it didn't disfigure my face as they thought. See, Jesus still wins. After that, the light bulb went off in my head and I actually seen my ex for who he was, and I left and never looked back.

Over the years with my ex, there had been many days when I wanted to leave, and many days that I left, but I didn't have the strength to stay gone. He would always follow me or call like crazy to get me back after the fight. I was young and didn't know any better, and I would go back to the same things, hoping that something had changed. All to find out things had only changed for a few weeks.

I'm not trying to tell you to leave your mate, but if he's hitting on you, it probably won't stop until you're all broken up and he has you where no one else would even look your way. Then off he goes again to control some other woman.

There hath no temptation taken you but such as is common to man: but God is faithful, who will not suffer you to be tempted above that ye are able; but with the temptation also make a way of escape, that ye may be able to bear it.

~1 Corinthians 10:13

If you let the Lord lead, and you follow, He will bless you. God gave me a husband who loved me for me. He didn't care about the scares, he only cared for me and my kids. I'm so blessed and grateful for this great man that He has given me.

REMOVE THE STONES

2

REMOVE THE STONES OF FEAR

Has anyone every offended you, and you just couldn't seem to shake it? Especially when you were only trying to be of great help to them, all to find out they were really trying to take you out.

I can remember opening our door to some people who we truly tried to help until they could get in a place of their own, settle down, and get on their feet. In the midst of my husband and I housing these people of God, days turned into weeks and weeks turned into 9 months. And let me say, they were pastors and a family of six. We never asked them for anything, and I have never told people about what happened until now.

My husband worked offshore, and we had just moved into our home. We had been there for maybe a month or two, but there was plenty of room in our home. And besides, my husband was always offshore. Well, my church family at the time moved in and all hell broke loose in my home.

I never thought that my spiritual fight would be the way it was. See, sometimes people can get a complex about you helping them, and that was the case. I asked over and over for the kids to eat in the kitchen, but even that was a fight. I felt if my kids could eat in the kitchen, well so could theirs. Another fight was they didn't look like they were trying to move forward, nor were they looking for a place to stay.

I could remember the pastor's wife coming into my bedroom and sitting on my floor talking to me. Every time she came in, she would begin to tell me the same story, over and over again. Until one day, she came in to sit and tell me that same story, but after she began talking, a spirit walked in the room, walked to the side of my bed, and disappeared.

I couldn't believe what I was seeing with my eyes and I asked her did she see that. Well, she just kept right on talking as if I had never said a word. God began to show me that she was releasing a spirit of fear in my room and I didn't know what to do because these were my leaders at the time. And yes, on this journey when the light is turned on, it will draw all types of insects and bugs; darkness is always drawn to the light.

While I was without my husband when he was away, I would fast study, and was always praying. But somehow the enemy came in, even after I saw what was going on. It still had me in a fearful state.

Faith cannot work when fear is present. Yes, even with me fasting there were things I didn't cover like backbiting, talking about the wrong things that they were doing, and judging. So, guess what? That left me uncovered. Some would say, *well, look how they didn't help you.*

I would go out to cut my grass while my husband was away working, while there were two adult men and two teenage boys in the house who wouldn't lift a finger. With me being offended, that fear was able to come in and take root in my spirit. Again, faith will not operate when fear is present.

Now I have a spirit of fear in my house, and I was really alone, because these people were against me for helping them. Wow! That was a lesson learned.

When that ninth month came, I was so afraid to ask them to leave, but if I had listened to my husband, they would have been gone by now (ladies listen to your husbands). Even after helping and asking them to leave, we let them use our car, still just trying to be of help, but they returned about a week later and brought it back. Still, it was the wrong thing to do.

The pastor didn't want anything to do with my family after my husband asked them to leave. Not only that, but I was also at my mother-in-law's house when they left, and we came back to maggots on the outside of the house. These were some of the biggest maggots I had ever seen, a den full of flies. I remember asking my nephew to bring some fly spray to my house, and he did. We sprayed the spray in that den and not one of those flies died. I went into prayer and fasting and eventually they disappeared, but after all that the fear was still there. I was in a cave for a few years after. I really didn't want to deal with any church folks.

A few months later I was sleeping, and I dreamt

of a spider that came down over me and bit my top lip. Well, to my surprise, I woke up with a swollen lip. I knew that I was being fought spiritually and still did not have a mentor, but I have to give honor where honor is due. Jan and Paul Crouch of TBN were very helpful to me and my husband. I was on this journey with the Holy Spirit and Benny Hinn. The Holy Spirit is a teacher, a guide, an instructor, a director, and a comforter.

You know, sometimes you can think that something is gone, but in the back of your mind it's still there. Well, that's what I went through until I was sick and tired, of being sick and tired. So, one day I said to the Lord, *I see, and I know everything that was done to me, but I can't carry this load anymore and I need for it to be gone.*

I became desperate, and I needed that fear to be gone from my life, and God did it. But it was only because I gave it up. See, I had never realized that I was holding on to it. I wanted it gone, but I had to release that thing from me.

REMOVE THE STONES

3

REMOVE THE STONES OF BITTERNESS

I could remember many years ago going through the stages of bitterness. My kid's dad and I had joint custody of our kids. I knew that I was in a pretty dark season in my life. As the years went on and my oldest child turned sixteen, she became rebellious all in one day. I don't know if you have seen anything like this before. But one day she refused to come home from her visit with her dad.

I was a young mother. My mother had passed some years before and I was lost. I didn't know what to do, and I didn't understand. I just didn't see it coming at all. I went to my daughter's grandmother's house, where she was at the time, and I said, "Come on. I'm here to get you."

And she said, "No."

My Lord. I felt like my heart had dropped clean

out of my body. I was in shock and didn't know what to do. After all, she was sixteen and at her grandmother's house up the street from her dad's house. We begin to have words and went back and forth about her getting in the car. She ran in to her grandmother's house and I ran behind her. I was falling on the ground trying to get to my child, because I knew what could happen to her out there.

You know sometimes, a broken heart can bring in the spirit of bitterness and things you were not anticipating to happen, happens. It might start off as a broken heart, but remember, spirits never come alone, they always come with the intention to enter in with other stronger spirits (Matthew 12:43-45).

And let me add, about a year in a half later my second born did the exact same thing to me, and even with that I never saw it coming, because I thought I was a great mother, I had my kids in church and I was now living for the Lord. With that said, I just knew that all was well even though I was still grieving for my baby who had left me and now my other daughter too.

My Lord, I thought to myself, *I must be a bad*

mother, my kids have left me and they really don't want to be face to face with me. Lord, I thought to myself, *what have I done wrong.*

I was in a very low place for a few years. How can my kids, who I raised, now see me as a bad person? The enemy gave me tormented dreams almost every night concerning their safety. I was fasting and praying during that time, and my kids still didn't want to return home. I began to beat up on myself. I couldn't figure things out at all, even though in my mind I was saying *I'm going through this because of the love I have for God*, somehow hoping that things would change. Well, it never did.

It was about seven years later when I sat done with one of my daughters and I asked, "Was I a horrible mother to you guys?" Yes, believe it or not I was still silently suffering from not knowing why my kids decided to leave me.

To my surprise, my daughter said, "Mom, it was nothing that you did. It was on us. We wanted to be grown, and we knew if we stayed with our dad, we could do anything that we wanted, because he was never home, and all our cousins and friends could come over and hang out whenever they wanted to. It had nothing at all to do with you."

Sometimes we get bitter over things that we can't control, even when we thought we had control and lost it with our kids. Mothers and fathers don't give up on your kids because they choose the other parent. There is always a reason for it. It doesn't necessarily mean that you've done something wrong to your kids. Don't allow bitterness to come in because of the things you see with your natural eye, we must get in the spirit to see what's really going on. And I want you to know the plans and the plots of the enemy will not prevail if you keep your hands and heart in God's hand and seek him for instruction.

One day, one of my bishops from a church I used to go to said as he was preaching, "Let those hardheaded kids go. Why stay up all night worried about them? They are going to do whatever they want until their eyes are open."

That sermon changed my life.

They that wait upon the Lord shall renew their strength, they shall mount up with wings as an eagle, they shall run and not be weary, walk and not faint. ~Isaiah 40:31

Even when things are not going right, pray for the strength to make it through and you will get through. Sometimes things take a little time. It doesn't happen overnight. Please don't be bitter, get better and know that in the midst of it all, God is on your side even when everything seems silent.

REMOVE THE STONES

4

REMOVE THE STONES OF JEALOUSY

Jealousy can go undetected in the beginning. Sometimes that thing can hide in a person but know and understand that it could only hide for so long. Jealousy always shows itself. You know why? Because it can only hide for a season. It's a horrible spirit to have. Jealousy kills, it drives people to murder in real life and spiritually.

Just as with Cain and Abel, it was jealousy that caused Cain to kill his brother. Sometimes we kill our brothers and our sisters in Christ, in the workplace, and our blood sisters and brothers, not with a physical weapon, but with something much harder to hold, and that is our tongue.

But the tongue can no man tame; it is an unruly evil, full of deadly poison. Selah,

~James 3:8

Take into consideration that we, being human, are made in the image of God, being just a little lower than the angels, can tame animals, and beast of the field, but the tongue no man can tame. We can find ourselves in life upset and cursing everyone who we think crosses us. Everyone will not always agree with you, everyone will not always like you, and everyone will not always see the best in you. You must know who you are on this journey called life.

Be not deceived God; God is not mocked; for whatsoever a man soweth, that shall he also reap. ~Galatians 6:7

I can remember being in a place in my life where I was jealous, and not really understanding what that spirit held. It is a poison. You can't grow with jealousy, and you surely can't love with jealousy. We all know that Jesus is love, so no Love—no God, point blank.

Some things we find ourselves jealous of are not even worth it. A coworker doing better than us, a sister in Christ seems to be doing better than us, or our neighbor prospering, and we start to wonder what's going on with us. We think to ourselves, *what have I done wrong?* Looking as if the more I try to do right or live in an honest way, things never go right.

The enemy is always lurking and trying to make you feel less than others, that's how he works. He's full of tricks and illusions. He can paint a false picture before you that looks so real, just as he does in this day in time on Facebook (FB). FB is great in some ways, but in many ways it's terrible for people, especially jealous people. We look at the world and before you know it, you want to be in their shoes. *If I could only get a head start as they did...*, is the thing we think to ourselves.

We never know the cost of someone else's success or anointing. The grace that God has placed on a person's life is for them to endure their trial, their test, and their tribulations. So, can we seriously say if we were really in their shoes, we could endure their heart aches or their trouble, of being raped, molested as a child, abandon, or abused as a child or adult?

I'm saying all of that to say, you never really know the cost of someone else's oil/anointing. Life can sometimes get very loud, and not everyone makes it out of their situations. Many people lose their minds and can't seem to recover from the tragic moment in their life that left them numb, in some cases, and in other cases functionable before people but destroyed in their daily life behind closed doors. We are looking at the outer appearance and have the nerve to be jealous of our coworkers, friend, neighbors, or just people who we see on a daily basis and never really know the truth or the hardship that they went through.

Before we become jealous of a person, we need to know their story, then maybe we could appreciate them more.

For where envying and strife is, there is confusion and every evil work. ~James 3:16

These are the things that stem from jealousy, jealousy comes with friends. How to be free from these things is in Hebrews 12:1…

Wherefore seeing we also are compassed about with so great a cloud of witnesses, let us lay aside every weight, and the sin which doth so easily beset us, and let us run with patience the race that is set before us. ~Hebrews 12:1

If we stay in our lane and focus on our lane, we have no space to overlap into other lanes. When jealousy wants to rise in you, shut it down, cast it out, and fill your mind and thoughts with the pleasant things of life. Think about how you made it through your stormy days. And for those of us who feel like we don't have stormy days, well all I can say is, if you live long enough trials will come. Don't be beguiled, but grow and help someone else to grow.

REMOVE THE STONES

5

REMOVE THE STONES OF ANGER

Anger can be something serious in our lives. I could remember being angry in my childhood and growing up with a little anger, but later on it grew to be a really big anger that turned into rage. Again, these spirits never come alone, they are always with friends seeking resident in our space. That's why when we are loosed from these spirits, or free from them, with must fill that space, because that spirit is always trying to come back into our dwelling.

I remember as a child getting angry and wanting to fight back whenever my family was fighting with a neighbor. But my true anger came when I had to fight in a relationship. It was a horrible relationship. We would fight and in the middle of fighting or after the fight was over, he forced himself on me and made me interact with him in intercourse. This went on for years and years, even to the point of him locking me up in the house the day after the fight so I couldn't leave him while he was at work.

The things we take as a young lady and wanting to live that adult life. I had kids at a young age and somehow felt trapped. I would tell anyone today, *no means no!* I don't care who it is, husband or wife, it doesn't matter. I know that we are to submit to our mates, but not if your being abused. Abuse is not God—at all—and don't allow the enemy to fool you. God does not wish for you to be beat on, neither does He want you to beat on anyone.

As the years passed, my anger grew, and before I knew it, I was operating in rage. I got to the point where I was ready for a fight. I didn't bother anyone, but if they said anything to me out of the way, I was ready at all times. I was just pure angry, and I would ask the Lord: *Why you are letting him do me this way?* Now I didn't know God like that, but I had heard about Him from church and from my mother, but I was still talking to Him even when I didn't know Him.

There were times when I left that relationship after a fight and I would allow him to come right back into my life the next week. Really. Yes, I thought that was love. I couldn't see that after God made a way of escape for me that I went back time and time again.

As things festered in my life, my kids were growing and coming of age and they could see things and remember them. I would get so mad that I would start cursing like a sailor, and every word that came out my mouth was crystal clear and loud cursing. People could hear me all the way down the road, cutting up. That thing grew on me.

Could you imagine the anger that was bottled up inside of me and it was growing, and me being so very young? I didn't know how to get rid of it, or even if I wanted to get rid of the anger. It was a part of my life now and was embedded really deep. Certain words or jesters caused me to act, or should I say react, a certain way. It was horrible; it caused me to be stagnated in life and truly not able to grow or move forward to get out of the bad relationship.

One day on my way home from work after working a 16-hour shift, I opened up my heart and Jesus came in. My life has never been the same, from many years ago up until today. That is what Jesus will do to you: He will save you, clean you up, and make you look like you had never done that thing before in your life.

Therefore, if any man be in Christ, he is a new creature: old things are passed away; behold, all things are become new. ~2 Corinthians 5:17

When all things had become new, I was able to get some things done. I was able to go back to school and get my GED, go to Cosmetology school and complete it, open up a hair salon, and go to bible college. I got an Associate's Degree, and I could have gone further, but I stop there for a minute.

These are things I couldn't have gotten when I was in that angry place in my life. Why do I say that? Because I tried to get my GED, and it just didn't work, but when I came to know Christ, as my personal Lord and Savior, my life changed. I filled that place where anger used to live, with joy and self-love for myself.

6

REMOVE THE STONES OF SELF RIGHTEOUSNESS

I can remember a time in my life, maybe after a few years of being saved, when I thought everything I had learned and everything that I knew about church and Christ was the only way. I was what they called a *Holy Roller,* fire and brimstone type of Christian.

Everything I learn I thought was right, and it just went one way. Always lifting up what I knew and not really wanting to hear what others had to say about many things. I actually felt like I had no room for mistakes. Boy, was I ever so wrong. It was my way or the highway. I missed out on so much of my family, friendships, and so much more.

I really thought that I was living a great life in God until the Holy Spirit began to reveal to me that I was in the wrong and that I had to make it right. Not only for me, but for the people who were standing by waiting on me, my kids and generations to come. See, God loves us so much that He will not leave us in a jacked-up state of mind, not unless that is something that we want and don't allow Him in to change us. The Lord will always show you yourself first before He shows anyone else. He always gives us a chance to make it right with Him and also with others.

That's why when I see a self-righteous spirit on someone I can identify, because I have been there myself and had I already walked in those shoes. Being right all the time is not what life is all about. Having to be the only one with the answer is not what it is about. Winning an argument is not what life, or the kingdom, is all about. Being faultless in my own mind was not what life was all about. Trying to walk around free from sin was not what the kingdom was all about.

For all have sinned and fallen short of the glory of God. There is no perfect flesh, but there is a perfect spirit. ~Romans 3:23

Some people also have certain things that they call righteousness to fit their lifestyles, it's called adjustable righteousness, which means it fits me whenever I want it to, as if God's just going to go along with that mess. Yes, I said it–*that mess*. Self-righteousness is only pure evil. We walk around condemning others and when people aren't looking we do the same things that the world is doing. Living any kind of way before God. We call it righteous when it comes down to us and our situation, but it's fire and brimstone on others.

Well, guess what eventually happens when we don't take heed of God's correction? He pulls the cover off of us and exposes the life that we're really living. Then we see people caught in the act of adultery, pregnancy, murder, gossip, slander, and whoredom in the church. Yes, I said it—*in the church*.

God gives all of us a chance to get things right. He is a loving God; He is an awesome God. He loves in spite of the things we do; I call Him a God of another chance, and that goes on and on, until He has to use force with us because we are ignoring the Word and are doing what we want to do.

The only way to get rid of self-righteousness is to own your mistake, take heed when the searchlight is on you, release the junk from your spirit and repent, keep it moving, and thank God that He loves you enough to show you yourself.

7

REMOVE THE STONES OF HURT

Hurt can cause a grave yard death in your life. Hurt can also cause one to let a dead man rule from the grave. I have lived and learned that people have been through different types of hurt caused by many people who came into their lives, some who they let into their lives, and others who forced themselves into their lives.

I have seen hurt come from misunderstandings, molestation, abuse, rape, and many other things. I have seen some people so hurt that they never really recovered and turned to drugs. Some 30 years later and they are still on drugs and I have seen some die on drugs.

I have seen some people who had been raped 30 and 40 years ago, but they are still grieving from their innocence being taken from them as a child.

They blame themselves, although it had nothing to do with them and everything to do with that sick individual who violated them. Most of the time that person was fulfilling the lust of the flesh. Some people in their minds can't find a way of escape, though God has already made the way for them.

Hurt can cause a person to come to a total stop and be stagnated and not want to move on in life. It also leaves people with a suicide state of mind. There are women, men, boys, and girls who are going through and have already been through these things. Some recover and some don't.

I know people who have been hurt and can't let it go; I know people who have had an abortion after abortion and can't seem to forgive themselves. I have seen women who were up for a promotion and their coworker got it instead of them, and it left them damaged. I have seen people hurt because of race or simply because their skin was not light enough. I have seen husbands and wives destroy their families because of the hurt that someone cause to the other, and they couldn't seem to get passed it.

Sometimes we have to step outside of ourselves

and review the circumstances around us. I found that life is full of choices. We have to learn how to navigate in this thing called life, things will not always be good, and it won't always go the way that we want them to go.

I always say it takes a lifetime to know a person. You can be with someone for years and not know them. That's why I always ask God to show me people's hearts. Hurt people, hurt people, and damage others because of the hurt that no one can see in the heart of man.

Hurt can cause a person to wake up in places they never thought that they would be. Hurt people have a stench to them that they carry. It's just like carrying an infectious disease, sometimes it's as if it's airborne, it can go from person to person.

Have you ever been in the company of people and they could speak or act a certain way and you notice that the entire mood changes? Then you find yourself speaking just like them? Corrupted communication ruins good manners. It's very true, and it's the word of God. That's why it's important to observe those around you.

Try the spirit by the spirit and know if it's of God. ~John 4:1

Have you ever met someone, and they looked to be older and mature until they open their mouths, and you hear nothing but a child speaking in a grown-up body? In some cases, we need to mature, and in other cases people are stuck where they got hurt in their past. They are still that 16-year-old girl who got raped; they are still that 15-year-old man who was abused; they are still that young father who was 17 years old and had to raise a child, and so much more.

Sometimes we need the help of God, and the professional who has already been trained for this situation. And because we speak with professionals doesn't make us crazy. That's the problem. No one wants to talk to a psychological professional to bring about the help that is needed for them to move forward in life.

We can never measure the amount of hurt someone is feeling. Sometimes hurt can cause illnesses to come upon your body. Many people don't agree, but I know it to be a fact. I have seen it happen to people, especially men, and now I look at things differently, from other perspectives. There are so many things going on in the world today, and it's time to know who you are and Whose you are.

REMOVE THE STONES OF HURT

Arise and shine for thy light has come and the glory of God has risen upon you. ~Isiah 60:1

I found a way out of the hurt and pain of my past, and that was getting to the point in my life where I would read the word, but God said that was not enough. I had to conceive the word of God. We must get free so we can help others get free. Those who can set a captive man free are only someone who has been captive themselves.

In most cases, I don't want people who have no experience to lead me into anything. I can remember getting involved in a project, and I thought, because I had done all my research on this project, it would work out just the way that I planned it. Wrong. That didn't happen. I thought because of the homework that I had done and my research, it all would work out as planned, even after counting the possible loss that could happen.

Well, let me put it this way. It was a great loss, and many people were affected by it. And it was all because sometimes you can have info that sounds good, but if you haven't walked it out yourself, far in advance before you bring others in, things can get really bad, really fast. There is a process before the promise. Always walk a situation out first before you bring others in.

Cast your cares upon him, for he cares for you.
~1 Peter 5:7

That scripture alone says a lot. We must fight for our freedom. Jesus came to set the captive free. There is such freedom in the Lord no matter the problem and no matter what your facing, God is able to do all things but fail. He can't fail us.

For my yoke is easy, and my burden is light.
~Matthew 11:30

8

REMOVE THE STONES OF FALSE HUMILITY

Having a spirit of false humility can be a dangerous thing. Being fake is totally a lie. There is no if, and, or butts about it. Telling someone you love them with words from your mouth but showing them something different in your action is not good. I learned that false humility could get a person in a real bad stink, because eventually, others will know because of what a person says or how one reacts to people can tell on them.

I can remember being around people who I loved, and who I thought loved me, but in reality, it was fake love. I can remember being in a place with some people who acted as if it was a 'play' with false humility. I mean, they really had me fooled and lots of others as well. They were back stabbers, slanders, liars, thieves, and much more, too much to name. We all know people who lie just to hear themselves talk, but then we have those who make up things concerning people, those who create difficulties for others and for themselves, and they try to make it look like an honest mistake. That's false humility.

I have seen it and I too have also stood in this place of false humility. Things as simple as, *Hi how are you sister, or brother*, and I couldn't stand the sight of them and they could not stand the sight of me. But we laughed and hugged, and said, *Love you sis,* and love was so far away from us. The type of person I was at that time was few with words, but we all faked things at some point in time in our lives.

I have seen leaders fake with members they couldn't stand the sight of, but they put on a smiley face and act as if they were really interested in that person and what they were doing or what they stood for, but it was false humility.

Have you ever seen a wolf in sheep's clothing? That's false humility. Being humble is being mild-mannered, having control of yourself, modest, meek, lowly, abase, respectful, without pride, peace with themselves or with others.

REMOVE THE STONES OF FALSE HUMILITY

I have met some of the most fake leaders who demonstrated false humility, and I would pray and ask God to *please help me*, because I didn't want that spirit to be a part of my life. And yes, I do mean a part of my life.

See, in some cases, we carry things for so long that it becomes who we are. Pretenders become who we are, fakeness becomes who we are, lies become who we are, authentic fake becomes our norm. Slanders, thieves, and lies become our character and we convince ourselves that we are telling the truth when our truth is really based on a lie—wow.

I have seen people whose appearance seems to be as if they were so meek in spirit before certain people, and behind closed doors, they are prideful and won't take anyone's advice. They think their way is the only way. Conceited, arrogant, and pure hardheaded, which eventually gets us nowhere. When they are before people you would think that they love you and that they care, but in reality, there is no truth to their actions behind closed doors. And not only that, if you continue to watch, you will know the truth about someone.

REMOVE THE STONES

We must get rid of all hypocrite spirits that are within. And no one has to tell you about what's in you, because you are the first to know, you may want to be in denial, but you are the very first to know what you battle with, even if you're not able to speak or confess that thing to your brother, sister, friend, or acquaintance. You must be ready to release all negative things that want to dwell within you. If you don't release the fakeness, it will grow in you and other things will begin to take root within you as well.

Believe in yourself, then you can believe in others. Always know when you think you smart there is always someone smarter—always. This is why we come to these places in our lives, because we either are trying to prove ourselves to people because of our insecurities, we want to be accepted by people; we want to look smart to people, or we want to be what others need or want in life.

Know that you can't be everything to everybody, point blank. You fill the area that you're to be in someone's life and leave the other areas alone that others are to fill. That way the stress is not on you and you don't have to go into a lying place, or a place of falsehood.

REMOVE THE STONES OF FALSE HUMILITY

You don't have to be superior to others, find yourself and just be social with others. Believe it or not, some people love to see you make a fool of yourself and know that you're not going to always be right about everything. You may come close, but never always.

We have to be ever so careful because we carry generations within us. I know some people who have truly destroyed generations of their families because of their false humility. I have seen people come to visit older people who are set in their ways and before that person can get outside the door they started saying very evil things about people, but to their face they were smiling and offering them food from their kitchen. That's false humility. This thing is true.

I have also seen generations perverted because of it. The things that we do and say do indeed have meaning to them.

> *But those things which proceed out of the mouth come forth from the heart; and they defile the man. For out of the heart proceed evil thoughts, this teaching of doctrines the commandments of men. ~Matthew 15:18-19*

This is what the word says about fake people, and this is the thing that eventually takes place in a people's life. This is the fruit of false humility. Turn, remember to repent, and move forward in Christ. You may struggle with these things, but God is able to move all of them. As you release them, He takes them and throws them all away. All you have to do is keep going and don't let anything stop you from pressing forward. Think about your kids and your kid's kids, and remember generations are in you.

9

BE DESPERATE TO REMOVE THE STONES

We are in a season of our lives where we must be desperate to remove the stones that block our sight of God. Whether it's fear, bitterness, jealousy, anger, self-righteousness, hurt, offense, false humility, and many more. During these times, these are things that stagnate us in our everyday life as well as our Christian walk with God.

With these stones in the way we, as well as their offspring, can't see clearly. We have allowed people to cause us to stumble. And if you truly think about it, the ones who get to us are the people who have been rejected, offended, put down, are shut up in some way, shape, form, or fashion.

If I thought about people and what they thought about me, this book wouldn't exist right now, because they never knew, nor did they understand, me and what I was called to do. I had to learn the hard way. You know, I have always heard older people say, *bought sense is better than any.* Now I understand why they say that. When you pay a price for what you've been through, you begin to think before you act, and you really begin to take notice of a thing before you act.

The Lord began to show me about desperate people in the bible going to desperate measures to get their stuff. Can you be honest with yourself, not with people but with yourself first, and say I really need to change some things in my life?

This is what I had to do over the past, almost 18 years. Yes, it's been a journey, but God has kept me through it all and delivered me from them all, and it all came from wanting to be accepted and wanting to belong to a group of people. But God said, *I'm all you need to be affirmed.*

You know what happened almost every time I wanted and sought for others' emotional support or encouragement? God would allow the enemy to get busy, until one day I sat quietly, and I heard God say, *I called you. Not man. Why are you seeking to be excepted by man?* He reminded me of what He told me from the beginning: *Put not your trust in man because they are only human, they will fail you.*

God will never fail you. I was seeking to be approved by man when God had already approved me before the foundation of the earth. I get happy when I think about who God is and who He has been to me. Sometimes we forget about the call because we are so caught up in the church, the four walls church, not the church within us, but the church of man- and man-made things.

I learned a valuable lesson over the years, and it took a minute for me to really understand everything. Sometimes we can be preaching, teaching, praying, prophesying and be jacked up in our spirit man. But God loves us so much that He will put the light on us, and He orders our private world. You know the things that no one really knows about us. Those private struggles, and He says, *I'm going to bless you, but you must get rid of this and that.*

See, God knows the very intent of your heart,

you know how some people ask a question, but they ask the question and then they answer it too because in reality the intent was to ask it so they could answer it to let someone know of what they were thinking? Funny right? Everyone knows someone like that. But see, the Lord knows before you can even ask or say, so we must be careful with how we handle things, people, and situations.

I've seen some people start a conversation about someone that was not good, and then they shut up to let others do the talking. The others didn't pay attention, but guess who does pay attention? God does.

The heart is deceitful above all things, and desperately wicked: who can know it.

~Jeremiah 17:9

Still, even though they started it and said a word or two then shut up, the point is they knew what they were doing when they started the conversation. That's why the word says keep your conversation holy, then you won't have to worry about things being said or done.

Now are you willing to be desperate for the things of God? The Story of Tamar in the book of Genesis starts in chapter 38:1, as we all know but just to paraphrase. Tamar got desperate for what was promised to her. She was promised a thing by her father-in-law. God destroyed her husband, Er, because he was so wicked. So, Judah told his other son, Onan, to give his brother's wife his seed, and because Onan said to himself: *I'm not going to give her seed*, because the seed wouldn't be his and he pulled out and spilled it on the ground. God seen that he too was wicked, and He killed him as well.

Then Judah said Tamar would remain a widow at thy father's house until Shelah, his youngest son, becomes grown, unless he also dies prematurely, as his brothers did.

She went back to her father's house to wait on the youngest son to mature to give her a seed. But the youngest son was now grown, and what Judah had promised her wasn't happening.

See, Tamar was looking at her promise and she knew in her heart that it was not going to happen because Shelah was now grown, and it was not even being mentioned of.

Judah's wife had died, and he went up to his sheep shears in Timnath with his friend Hirah.

REMOVE THE STONES

Someone told Tamar Judah went up Timnath. By this time, she was so desperate for what was promised to her that she would do whatever it took to get it. So, she took off her widow's clothes, and she put on a veil, and wrapped herself and sat where she could be seen by Judah.

Now, as a woman, we all know about a veil wrap. That's something that can be revealing, but yet you are still covered—Selah.

When Judah saw her, he thought that she was a harlot because her face was covered. Sometimes you must disguise yourself to get your promise. That means you don't have to arrive sounding the alarm saying, "I'm here! Look at me, I have arrived!"

He asked Tamar to come into her and she said what will you give me? He said I will send a kid from my flock, but she said I can't just take your word. See, she had already been lied to by Judah, so she says give me something else, pledge something so that I can be sure of you and what you said you would do for me, and he said ok.

She said give me thy signet, and hid bracelet, and his staff. She was making sure there was no mistaking things. Tamar was so desperate that she did what she felt was needed to be done for her to receive her seed.

He laid with her, and she conceived that day. Tamar took off her revealing clothes and put her widow garments back on and she went back home. Judah sent the kid by his friend the Adullamite to receive his pledge from the woman, but she was gone. They asked the men of that town where is the harlot who was by the wayside, and these men said there was no harlot here in this place.

Judah said let her keep the things lest we be shamed, but after about three months Tamar was showing and all the people were gossiping about her saying she had laid with some man, living any kind of way, and now she's caught.

Judah said bring her to me so that she can be burnt.

And the daughter of any priest, she profane her father: she shall be burnt with fire.

~Leviticus 21:9

So, Tamar sent to her father-in-law, told the man those things belong to the person I am pregnant for. She said here it is, now you think about who these things belong to. So, Judah said, *these things belong to me.* And just like that, everything was in Tamar's favor. She did what she thought was best for herself. At this point, she didn't need for others to tell her how to handle things. She got desperate for herself to get what was promised to her.

Judah said, *Yes, these things belong to me and yes you have been more righteous than me because I withheld what I had promised to her I told her she could have my youngest son seed.* Judah never came through with that promise, and Judah slept with her no more. It was just that one time and not only did she conceive, but she got double for her trouble. She had twins in her womb.

That's what God will do for you. If you can get desperate for the things of God, you shall have double. Go through your process but come out learned, lived, and laughing. Don't stop moving, keep on paving the way forward for the younger generation, be an example of coming through your process to get to your promise.

We don't have to stop living or have to stop being saved because of the pains of life. I always say if you think you have never done anything

BE DESPERATE TO REMOVE THE STONES

wrong or judge anything wrong, you just haven't lived long enough, but we have to learn how to overcome adversity in our lives. And remember, if things sit in your spirit man for more than three days, and that thing begins to grow and take root inside of you, than you could end up in a worse situation in days, weeks, months, and years to come. So, kill it, because if you don't kill it you will serve it.